~STONE & MARBLE~

STONE & MARBLE

Penelope O'Sullivan

MetroBooks

MetroBooks

An Imprint of the Michael Friedman Publishing Group, Inc.

First MetroBooks edition 2002

Library of Congress Cataloging-in-Publication Data available upon request.

ISBN 1-58663-532-8

Editor: Reka Simonsen
Art Director: Jeff Batzli
Designer: Jennifer O'Connor
Photography Editor: Valerie E. Kennedy
Production Manager: Camille Lee

Color separations by Fine Arts Repro House Co., Ltd.
Printed in China by C.S. Graphics Shanghai Pte., Ltd.

1 3 5 7 9 10 8 6 4 2

For bulk purchases and special sales, please contact:
Michael Friedman Publishing Group, Inc.
Attention: Sales Department
230 Fifth Avenue
New York, NY 10001
212/685-6610 FAX 212/685-3916

Visit our website:
www.metrobooks.com

TABLE OF CONTENTS

INTRODUCTION

Stone evokes many moods in the home. Strong and earthy, stone proclaims substance, permanence, and stability. In architecture, it recalls the relative safety and security of caves, our primordial homes built into mountains and hillsides.

From the pyramids of ancient Egypt to the medieval castles of Europe, stone figures prominently in the cultural and design history of Western civilization. Almost three millennia before the birth of Christ, the Egyptian pyramids were constructed in the desert like abstract man-made mountains. Originally sheathed in smooth white limestone, these kingly tombs reflected the blinding radiance of the desert sun. Visually, they connected the earth with the sky. Symbolically, they linked Pharaoh, the entombed ruler, with the sun god, Re, and immortality.

By the end of the sixth century B.C., the Greek temple became a dominant form in Western architecture. Raised on a platform, the typical temple housed an image of a victorious deity or sometimes an oracle in a *cella* (chamber) surrounded by rows of columns. The earliest temples were built of timber and sun-dried clay tiles, followed by temples of ashlar or hewn stone. By 525 B.C., the Greeks made temples out of local marble, which could be polished to a shine and carved with detailed scenes that were then painted. The public, barred from entering the *cella*, saw their temples from the outside only— as ranks of massive, weight-bearing columns supporting a heavy, ornamented roof. Ancient temple ruins still assert their dignity and authority over the rocky terrain of modern Greece.

During the eleventh century A.D., the Normans began building rocky fortifications, a Roman custom that had waned some four hundred years earlier. Stone was the dominant building material because it was strong, fireproof, versatile, and impenetrable. Stone castles, frequently situated on hilltops for passive defense, had slit windows and battlements to allow soldiers while in the relative safety of the fortifications to rain arrows on an approaching enemy.

A key building material for thousands of years, stone falls into three groups: igneous, sedimentary, and metamorphic. Igneous rock, such as granite and basalt, is formed by the solidification of magma (molten rock)

Opposite: THE CLASSICAL MOTIFS CARVED INTO THIS GRAY AND WHITE MARBLE MANTEL COMPLEMENT THE SMALL STONE SCULPTURES STANDING ON TOP OF IT. TALL VASES FILLED WITH LILIES SET AT EITHER END OF THE MANTELPIECE ACCENTUATE THE CREAMY, LIGHT COLOR OF THE MARBLE AND GIVE THE ARRANGEMENT A LOOK OF ELEGANT FORMALITY.

sandstone and limestone run the gamut from off white, gold, and gray to purple and pink. Limestone is a traditional building material in many parts of North America and Europe, and it is often used for flooring and garden walkways as rock that has been subjected to and changed by tremendous heat or pressure. Marble comes in myriad colors and has been a favorite of architects for centuries, although today it is most often used to lend a sense of elegance to interiors.

within the earth. Granite is tough, lasting, and weather- and water-resistant; it ranges in color from black to white, gray, and red. Granite is popular for use both outside and inside the home, where it appears on kitchen counters and backsplashes, fireplace mantels, and even bathroom tiles. Basalt can be blue, green, brown, or black. Sedimentary rocks, such as sandstone and limestone, are formed by the erosion of various substances. Sandstone is made from the sediment of eroded igneous stones, and limestone from shells and skeletons. The colors of

The fashion for stone has ebbed and flowed through the centuries. In recent years, however, we've witnessed a renewed interest in the use of stone and marble both inside and outside the home. These materials can be quite expensive, so often they are used only on the facade or in small but significant details such as mantels, doorways, and window frames. Today, stone or marble decorative items such astables and countertops bespeak the home-owner's desire for substance and style. Whimsical applications for stone and marble are evident in contemporary design, which takes a fresh look at old motifs and uses them in new ways.

Above: SEVEN OF THE ORIGINAL THIRTY-EIGHT FLUTED DORIC COLUMNS SURVIVE IN THE TEMPLE OF APOLLO AT CORINTH, WHICH WAS BUILT CIRCA 540 B.C. INDIVIDUALLY CARVED CAPITALS, COVERED IN A MARBLE-DUST STUCCO SKIN, TOPPED THE COLUMNS, WHICH SUPPORTED AN ENTABLATURE AND PITCHED ROOF. ORIGINALLY, BRIGHT RED AND BLUE PAINTS WOULD HAVE HEIGHTENED THE TEMPLE'S DECORATIVE APPEAL.

Above: LIGHT AND SHADOW ADD DRAMA TO THIS TROPICAL SETTING. THE LOGGIA, OPEN BUT PROTECTED FROM THE ELEMENTS, RELIES ON THE COARSE STONE WALLS OF THE HOUSE AND THE GENTLY TEXTURED STONE PATIO TO CREATE A RUSTIC RETREAT FROM THE HOT MIDDAY SUN.

FIRST IMPRESSIONS

A well-designed stone facade gives a house an aura of permanence, beauty, and stability. When made from locally quarried material, a stone facade can also tie a building into its immediate surroundings and geographic region. Local stone also has the advantage of costing less to transport to nearby building sites than imported stone.

The practice of using stone from nearby quarries is a very old one that still prevails today. The ancient Greeks patronized local quarries to construct their marble temples in the sixth century B.C. In the nineteenth and twentieth centuries, New York City architects built traditional brownstone townhouses of sandstone from quarries in New York state.

Old fieldstone farmhouses are abundant in rural Pennsylvania, while suburban housing developments in

the area maintain regional character with local fieldstone facing. This thin stone veneer applied to concrete block or frame construction evokes a rural feeling and gives the look of stone without the cost.

The English are masters of stone construction, and their talents are nowhere more apparent than in the hilly Cotswolds. This region of England includes Gloucestershire and parts of Avon, Warwickshire, and Worcester. Cottages, manors, palaces, and whole villages built of this indigenous limestone warm the landscape with their tawny hues. Indeed, this ubiquitous golden stone brings harmony and an enduring allure to the region. Different building stones come from other parts of Great Britain, including granite from Cornwall and flint from East Anglia.

Opposite: A FLAGSTONE FLOOR, STUCCO WALLS PAINTED GOLDEN YELLOW, AND COARSE STONE TRIM AROUND THE DOOR CREATE A WARM, SUNNY, INFORMAL COURTYARD SETTING. PLANTERS AND WINDOW BOXES FILLED WITH ANNUALS, CLIMBING ROSES, A TINY BED OF PURPLE AND BLUE DELPHINIUMS, AND A COMFORTABLE RUSTIC CHAIR ANIMATE THIS CHEERFUL SCENE. **Above:** STONE COLUMNS AND A SCULPTURE STAINED WITH AGE FORM THE PERFECT BACKDROP FOR COLORFUL GARDEN PLANTS. OLD STONE SOFTENS THE CONTRAST BETWEEN THE CLIMBER'S SCARLET BLOOMS AND THE PURPLE-FLOWERING SHRUBS. LUSH GREEN FOUNDATION PLANTS LOOK PERFECTLY NATURAL JUMBLED AGAINST THE RUGGED STONE WALLS.

Slate, another popular building material, is found around the world, including Canada, the United States, Europe, and Africa. Slate splits easily into thin slices. It is also hard, fine grained, and weather-resistant, making it an excellent choice for roofing tiles, wall shingles, and outdoor paths. Its various colors include gray, red, blue, olive, and light and dark green.

Sometimes only part of a facade is made of stone. A Palladian stone portico adds grandeur and formality to a building. It designates a formal entrance, especially in large dwellings where lesser entries are intentionally plain and do not attract attention. Stone trim enhances windows, doors, corners, rooflines, and outdoor stairways. Stone looks particularly attractive when it contrasts with surrounding building materials, such as red brick or painted stucco.

Stone persists outdoors. It lasts best, however, when used in a climate similar to the one where it was quarried. Unlike wood, concrete, and many other outdoor building materials, stone doesn't require painting or exterior finishes. Limestone facades need occasional cleaning, since

Above: Along with wood, two types of stone make up the facade of this country house, which blends naturally into the surrounding landscape. The facade's near symmetry accentuates the perception of stability created by an abundance of stone. Exaggerated stone trim brings levity to this rather staid building. A retaining wall that forms a transition between the lawn and the drive extends the earthy impact of stone into the garden.

heavy urban pollution and extreme weather conditions affect its appearance. To avoid leaks, exterior stonework also needs repointing when the mortar between individual stones decays. Local stone weathers well, mellowing with time and improving with age.

Marble has endured as an outdoor building material for thousands of years in the mild climate of Greece, but it cannot withstand the harsh climatic changes of northern countries. Still, marble is popular in cooler countries as an elegant addition to transitional areas, such as entrance halls and courtyards. Generous expanses of marble flooring can form a graceful segue from the rough, natural textures of the outdoors to the softer, more decorative surfaces of a home's interior. Even a small marble piece, such as a marble-topped table or console, can lend sophistication to a transitional space. Whether employed as the main building materials of a home or used simply as decorative accents, stone and marble create a sense of permanence and ageless beauty wherever they are used.

Above: TALL, CAREFULLY SHAPED EVERGREENS LINE THE MAIN PATH TO THIS HOUSE IN THE COTSWOLD VILLAGE OF ARLINGTON. THE TALL, FLAT-TOPPED TREES TOWERING OVER THE GARDEN WALL ECHO THE IMPOSING SYMMETRY OF THE ROOF'S TWIN GABLES. MOREOVER, THE ALTERNATION OF LIGHT STONE AND DARK FOLIAGE CREATES A VISUAL RHYTHM THAT CARRIES THE GAZE STRAIGHT TO THE FRONT DOOR, THE FOCUS OF THE FACADE.

Below: BRIGHT BLUE PAINTED TRIM BRINGS GAIETY TO THE LIMESTONE FACADE OF THIS HOUSE. THE FEELING OF WHIMSY AND SPONTANEITY IS HEIGHTENED BY A DOORYARD GARDEN FILLED WITH A JUMBLE OF PINK AND WHITE FOXGLOVES AND LARGE-LEAFED HOLLY-HOCKS, BOTH TRADITIONAL COTTAGE GARDEN FLOWERS. **Opposite:** THE SIMPLE GRAY LIMESTONE FACADE OF THIS FARMHOUSE SUITS THE INFORMAL LANDSCAPE SURROUNDING IT. EXUBERANT WISTERIA SPREADS OVER ONE END OF THE HOUSE, LINKING THE AUSTERE STRUCTURE TO ITS NATURAL SETTING.

Above: THE PECULIAR CHARM OF THIS MODEST COTSWOLD HOUSE DERIVES FROM ITS HARMONIOUS FACADE, WHICH IS COMPOSED OF INDIGENOUS GOLDEN LIME-STONE SET OFF BY EBULLIENT LANDSCAPING IN GREEN AND A RANGE OF HOT MAGENTA HUES. BECAUSE OF AN APPARENTLY IN-EXHAUSTIBLE SUPPLY OF COTSWOLD LIME-STONE, PALACES, MANORS, AND VILLAGE DWELLINGS IN THE REGION ARE BUILT OF THIS POPULAR AND ATTRACTIVE ROCK.

Opposite: Massive in scale, an imposing Palladian portico with four columns and a stone pediment containing an oculus (round opening) is central to the design of this grand and stately building. By projecting the portico out from the main structure, the architect has increased its importance and enhanced the drama of light and shadow on the facade.

Above: Stone becomes a theme that integrates the interior of this elegant building with the exterior. In the entrance hall, the stone floor looks glossy with age and wear. Stone floors stand up well to indoor use in high-traffic areas. The doorway combines different hues of stone—gray for the step, ivory for the capitals, and soft gold for the pilasters. Plants in contrasting shades of green enliven the home's classical stone facade and graveled courtyard.

Opposite: DECORATED WITH A COLLECTION OF ARCHITECTURAL FRAGMENTS AND A ROW OF BUSTS ON PEDESTALS, THIS GRACEFUL LOGGIA PROVIDES AN ESCAPE FROM THE HEAT OF THE DAY. THE LOGGIA, THE FRAGMENTS, AND THE BUSTS AND PEDESTALS ARE ALL MADE OF STONE, WHICH PROVIDES THE UNIFYING ELEMENT IN THIS SETTING. LAVISH, DROOPY VINES HANGING FROM THE TERRACE ABOVE SOFTEN THE FORMAL REGULARITY OF THE ARCADE. **Below:** VINES OVERRUN THIS GOTHIC RUIN, WHICH BEARS A MESSAGE IN ITS TRANSIENT BEAUTY: CIVILIZATIONS FADE, BUILDINGS CRUMBLE, AND TIME CONQUERS THE CONQUERORS. BECAUSE OF STONE'S DURABILITY, HOWEVER, THIS TRACERY HAS SURVIVED FOR SEVERAL HUNDRED YEARS.

Above: THIS SANDSTONE WINDOW BELONGS TO THE TOMBS OF KINGS AT BADA BAGH NEAR JAISALMER, INDIA. IT IS A FINE EXAMPLE OF THE STONE CARVER'S ART. STYLIZED NATURALISTIC DESIGNS CUT IN BOTH HIGH AND LOW RELIEF ENHANCE THE PLAY OF LIGHT AND SHADOW ON THE TOMB'S SURFACE.

Above: THE WHITE STONE WALLS AND TRIM OF THIS ITALIAN VILLA REFLECT THE WARMTH OF THE SUN. SMALL ROUND WINDOWS, KNOWN AS OCULI, FORM A BAND UNDER THE ROOF. ROUNDED STONE PEDIMENTS AND CARVED SHELLS CAP FRENCH DOORS, WHICH OPEN ONTO SMALL BALCONIES. LUSH GREEN PALMS AND BOUGAINVILLEA, A SCRAMBLING WOODY VINE WITH BRILLIANT PURPLE BRACTS, PAINT A PICTURE OF SULTRY SPLENDOR, ESPECIALLY WHEN CONTRASTED WITH THE WHITE FACADE AND CLOUDLESS BLUE SKY.

Opposite: FRAMED BY PALM FRONDS, A STUNNING VIEW AWAITS VISITORS TO THE STONE TERRACE AT VILLA TRITONE IN SORRENTO, ITALY. THE BUSTS ON STAGGERED POSTS REPRESENT FOREBEARS, SIGNIFYING AN ANCIENT LINEAGE AND THE CONNECTION BETWEEN PRESENT AND PAST. LIKE THEIR ROMAN ANCESTORS, URBAN ITALIAN ARISTOCRATS BUILT VILLAS TO RETREAT FROM HECTIC CITY LIVES INTO THE PEACEFUL EXISTENCE OF THE COUNTRYSIDE.

Left: An intricately carved stone doorway lies on the main axis of this villa's facade. Symmetrically placed palms and a central fountain in a rectangular reflecting pool reinforce this line of sight. The smooth white stucco walls of the building help cool the interior by reflecting the intense sunlight. **Above:** The simplicity of the smooth stone facade of this villa makes the architectural details of the building even more dramatic. A French door framed by an extremely tall Gothic arch opens onto a delicate latticed stone balcony. A gracefully twisting stone staircase punctuated with carved stone finials leads up to the massive front door.

Opposite: THE STONE ENTRANCE HALL OF THIS CASTLE EXUDES ELEGANCE. ITS COOL, NEUTRAL COLOR PROVIDES THE PERFECT BACKDROP FOR AN ELABORATE BLACK WROUGHT-IRON BALUSTRADE AND AN IMPOSING LIGHT FIXTURE OF THE SAME MATERIAL. A GLEAMING BRASS HANDRAIL AND SUNBEAMS PLAYING ON SMOOTH STONE SURFACES ADD DYNAMIC CONTRAST TO THE SETTING.

Below: THE SIMPLICITY OF PALE, UNADORNED STRIPED WALLS OFFSETS THE STRONG COLOR AND PATTERN OF THE TWO-TONE POLISHED MARBLE FLOOR IN THIS HALLWAY. THE PATTERN OF WHITE DIAMONDS EXTENDING FROM ROOM TO ROOM UNIFIES THE CONNECTING ROOMS AND DRAWS THE GAZE FROM ONE ROOM TO THE NEXT.

Above: A STYLIZED WAVE MOTIF IS THE SUBJECT OF THE DECORATIVE MOSAIC BELOW THE CHAIR RAIL IN THIS GRACIOUS ENTRYWAY. MADE OF SMALL STONE SQUARES IN DIFFERENT COLORS, THE DESIGN IS EMBEDDED IN MORTAR TO HOLD IT IN PLACE. ALTHOUGH THIS PATTERN IS SIMPLE, SOME MOSAICS HAVE THE COMPLEXITY AND RICHNESS OF FINE PAINTINGS. TRAVERTINE TILES COVER THE WALL UNDER THE BORDER AND PAVE THE FLOOR.

GATHERING SPOTS

In the family gathering areas of a home—living rooms, great rooms, family rooms, dining rooms, and kitchens—stone and marble can create a sense of coziness or of formality. At once earthy and sophisticated, these durable materials can be used to make stylish walls, hearths, floors, counters, and columns.

In a cottage, a rustic stone hearth can be cozy and intimate, while in a larger home, a carved stone mantel brings elegance and stability to the design. Rustic walls made of indigenous stone give communal living spaces a picturesque, natural appeal by creating a direct link between indoors and out. Walls of gleaming polished granite, travertine, or marble, on the other hand, form a

striking formal backdrop for art objects and add purity and calmness to a design scheme.

Load-bearing pillars of stone can replace interior walls in the social rooms. Pillars open up indoor space and allow circulation, making it easier to entertain large groups. These pillars or columns can seem formal in a living room, when given a lintel and proper entablature, or casual in a great room or family room, where stone stands up to the wear and tear of children, pets, and parties.

It makes good sense to install stone floors in public areas that get lots of traffic because stone wears well. Stone also makes it easy to wipe up spills, and only water and a sponge or mop are needed to clean away dirt.

Opposite: There are two ways to install a sink in a stone surface. In this case, a stainless steel sink has been set into a polished granite work top. This method requires cutting appropriate holes by means of templates. Then the edge of each hole must be ground and polished to look like the main surface of the countertop. In the other, less expensive method, the sink sits on top of the hole, eliminating the need for finishing the edges of the opening. **Above:** This luxurious look is created with taupe speckled granite, dark walnut-stained wood, and brass fixtures. The gleaming brass and light, polished granite reflect the sunlight coming through the small-paned windows. These reflective materials balance the visual weight of the dark wood. In contrast to the gleaming brass and granite, the cabinets have the rich elegance of antique furniture.

Decorative stone floors take many forms. They can be inlaid with stone in different hues to create the effect of an area rug against a solid colored background. A geometric pattern of black granite against a backdrop of beige travertine makes a simple but striking design. It's also possible to incorporate color and complexity into walls or floors with mosaics. These small squares of colored stone or marble can be laid to form patterns or pictures. Mosaic floors or walls can give a room a sense of antiquity.

The kitchen is the heart of the home, a living space for family and friends. Here, stone and marble stand out for their practicality. In the kitchen, a rough, natural stone floor of slate or blue limestone gives the room a rustic character. Slate, moreover, is easy to clean and impervious to water. Cold, smooth marble is an excellent surface for pastry making, while thick, polished slabs of granite make superb, scratch-free work tops. Used together, stone and wood produce a snug, comfortable environment. Stone works like a magnet to draw people together and create a natural gathering place.

Moreover, plain slate, stone, or marble floors look good in most decorating situations. Stone or slate flooring with strong, graphic patterns or bold colors can add elegance to a room, and work best when the rest of the decor is kept sleek and simple.

Above: PRACTICAL YET ELEGANT, POLISHED GRANITE SUITS MOST KITCHEN DECORS. THIS HIGH-TECH CONTEMPORARY KITCHEN HAS SLEEK COUNTERS OF POLISHED GRAY GRANITE, WHICH COMPLEMENT THE BRUSHED STEEL OF THE STOVE AND DISHWASHER. WHITE LAMINATE CABINETS AND SHINY CHROME APPLIANCES COMPLETE THE DECOR.

Opposite: WHEN DECORATING WITH STONE, YOU DON'T HAVE TO LIMIT YOURSELF TO ONE TYPE OR COLOR. THE KITCHEN SHOWN HERE HAS A SLICK, GEOMETRICALLY PATTERNED STONE FLOOR AND BACKSPLASH. THEY ARE OF A SIMILAR, HARMONIOUS DESIGN BUT ARE NOT IDENTICAL. PATTERNED STONE FLOORS LIKE THE ONE PICTURED HERE WORK BEST WHEN THEY DON'T COMPETE WITH CLASHING PATTERNS AND COLORS. BEYOND THE KITCHEN, A FIREPLACE MADE OF ROUGH STONE AND THICK MORTAR HAS AN ALTOGETHER DIFFERENT, RUSTIC APPEARANCE.

Opposite: THIS STONE-TOPPED COOKING ALCOVE SPARKLES WITH WIT AND SOPHISTICATION. THE CONTRAST BETWEEN THE TRADITIONAL CARVED MANTEL AND THE STAINLESS STEEL OVEN SET BENEATH IT WOULD CAPTURE THE IMAGINATION OF EVEN THE MOST JADED VISITOR. **Above:** IN THIS KITCHEN, POLISHED BLACK GRANITE WITH WHITE FLECKS HAS BEEN USED FOR THE COUNTERS AND BACKSPLASH. THE DRAMATIC GRANITE BLENDS WITH PALE YELLOW WALLS, BLOND WOODEN CABINETS, AND ABUNDANT GLASS FOR A SOPHISTICATED EFFECT. RUSTIC STONE FLOORING ADDS A RUSTIC ELEMENT TO THE SLEEK DESIGN.

Opposite: NATURAL MATERIALS BRING THIS SLEEK, PRACTICAL KITCHEN DOWN TO EARTH. IN MANY HOMES, THE KITCHEN IS NOT JUST FOR COOKING BUT ALSO FOR SOCIALIZING AND DINING. DESIGNING WITH NATURAL MATERIALS LIKE THE HONEY-COLORED WOOD AND POLISHED GRANITE SHOWN HERE AVOIDS THE STERILE LOOK THAT MAKES SOME KITCHENS LESS THAN WELCOMING.

Above: MARBLE HAS TRADITIONALLY BEEN FAVORED FOR MAKING PASTRY BECAUSE OF ITS COLD SURFACE. MARBLE IS POROUS AND RELATIVELY SOFT, HOWEVER, SO IT STAINS EASILY. THE KEY TO SUCCESS WITH MARBLE AS A GENERAL WORK SURFACE IS WIPING UP SPILLED LIQUIDS QUICKLY AND USING A CUTTING BOARD FOR CHOPPING AND SLICING, SINCE THOSE ACTIVITIES CAN DESTROY THE FINISH OF A BEAUTIFUL MARBLE COUNTER SUCH AS THIS.

Right: SUNLIGHT SATURATES THIS KITCHEN, WHICH FEATURES A DESIGN THAT GLOWS WITH WARMTH. STAINED WOOD AND GLASS ARE THE PREVALENT MATERIALS, BUT THE THICK GRANITE TABLETOPS IN TAWNY PINK, BLACK, AND WHITE ADD TO THE SENSUOUS, ORGANIC QUALITY OF THE ROOM.

Opposite: HUGE BOULDERS FORM ONE WALL OF THIS EXTRAORDINARY DINING ROOM. CHAIRS UPHOLSTERED IN LEATHER, A LONG PLANK TABLE, AND A HANDSOME NATIVE AMERICAN VESSEL FILL THE TIGHT ENCLOSURE, CREATING A SOPHISTICATED INTERPRETATION OF AN INDIGENOUS SOUTHWESTERN CAVE DWELLING.

Above: INFORMALITY IS THE KEYNOTE OF THIS LIVING ROOM DOMINATED BY A STURDY FIREPLACE OF COARSE STONES. KNOTTY PINE FLOORBOARDS, BLACK WICKER FURNITURE, AND A MANTEL, CEILING BEAMS, AND CORNER JOINTS MADE OF PEELED LOGS COMPLETE THE RUSTIC SPIRIT OF THIS ROOM.

Left: AN ANTIQUE CARVED STONE FIREPLACE ACCENTUATES THIS ROOM'S TRADITIONAL FURNISHINGS. DARK PANELED WALLS, AN ORIENTAL CARPET, SEVERAL OLD TRUNKS USED AS TABLES, AND A HUNTING PRINT ABOVE THE FIREPLACE PROVIDE CONTRASTING LUXURIOUS TEXTURES AND ACT AS EMBLEMS OF THE GOOD LIFE. **Above:** SUNLIGHT POURS THROUGH THE OPEN DOOR OF THIS DELIGHTFUL GREEN AND CREAM KITCHEN. A RUSTIC STONE FLOOR, SIMPLE PAINTED CABINETS, RUSH SEATED LADDER-BACK CHAIRS, AND A LONG PLANK TABLE CREATE A CLEAN COUNTRY LOOK.

Above: A MARBLE FIREPLACE FORMS THE CENTER OF THIS TRADITIONAL LIVING ROOM. THE PLAIN DESIGN OF THE FIREPLACE, ITS PALE GRAY AND WHITE HUES, AND ITS COOL, BROAD EXPANSE SERVE AS AN INDISPENSABLE COUNTERBALANCE TO THIS BUSY ARRANGEMENT OF PAINTINGS, ART OBJECTS, TERRA-COTTA POTS, MAHOGANY FURNISHINGS, AND A COUCH UPHOLSTERED IN BRILLIANT GREEN AND YELLOW.

Above: A TRADITIONAL CARVED MARBLE FIREPLACE BRINGS SUBSTANCE, STABILITY, AND ELEGANCE TO THIS AUSTERE BUT FORMAL INTERIOR.

THE DECOR RELIES MORE ON NEUTRAL COLORS AND EARTHY MATERIALS THAN ON FANCY DECORATIONS FOR IMPACT. THE DRAMATICALLY TALL

WINDOW LETS IN PLENTY OF SUNLIGHT AND A VIEW OF VERDANT TREES AND SHRUBS.

Above: This unusual table, comprised of individual stone blocks on a metal base, resembles a cobbled street. The coarse surface, accentuated by the fissures between the blocks, enlivens an otherwise plain seating area by introducing an element of the unexpected. **Opposite:** A wall of glass and a wall of stone serve to bring the outdoors inside this spacious living room. The pale stone used for the fireplace and surround adds to the light, airy feeling of the space, while the neutral palette and understated decor allow the striking view to be the main attraction.

Below: THE STONE FIREPLACE ADDS WELCOME TEXTURE TO THIS CASUAL, EASTERN-INSPIRED LIVING ROOM WITHOUT DISTRACTING ATTENTION FROM THE DRAMATIC PLANTS AND ART OBJECTS FILLING THE SPACE. **Opposite:** AN UNPAINTED STONE WALL ACCENTUATES THE FACT THAT THIS LOFT IS SEPARATE FROM THE LARGER SPACE, WHERE THE OTHER HALF OF THE SAME WALL IS PAINTED YELLOW. TAKEN TOGETHER, THE LOFT WALL, THE UNFINISHED WOOD FLOORS, AND THE PLAIN RAILINGS ENHANCE THE SIMPLE, RURAL DECOR.

Above: THE SENSUAL APPEAL OF THIS CONTEMPORARY LIVING ROOM COMES NOT FROM ITS COOL GRAY COLORS AND SIMPLE SHAPES BUT FROM THE CONTRAST OF TEXTURES. THE DEEP UPHOLSTERED ARMCHAIR COVERED IN A SOFT WOOL BLANKET LOOKS WARM AND INVITING, WHILE A VERTICAL STONE SCULPTURE AND TWO SIDE TABLES, BOTH CUBES OF COLD STONE, MAKE A DRAMATIC COUNTERPOINT TO THE WARM HARDWOOD FLOOR AND WOVEN GRASS RUG.

PRIVATE SPACES

Bedrooms and bathrooms are intimate places where we can relax and escape from the pressures of the world outside. Whether the decor you choose is lush and filled with creature comforts or spare and simply furnished, these rooms should inspire a sense of peace and harmony.

Bedrooms serve many functions, from the purely practical requirement for a sleeping space to the spiritual need for a place to dream. Stone and marble can be used to enhance the calm, soothing environment of the bedroom. Fireplaces are spots where a small amount of marble or stone can make a huge impact. In an elegant neoclassical home, marble surrounds and mantels can be carved into graceful motifs from the classical period, such as garlands, Greek keys, and eagles. In a country-style home, river rock or rough, quarried stone can add to the rustic ambience.

If you aren't lucky enough to have a fireplace, there are plenty of other ways to incorporate these timeless materials into the bedroom. Dressers and vanities can be topped with marble or granite, or a small table with a marble base can be added. Antique stores and flea markets often have pieces of architectural salvage that can make wonderful table bases. In the bedroom, a little stone or marble adds a lot of style.

In the bath, stone and marble have myriad applications because they are easy to clean and promote excellent sanitary conditions. Granite, marble, and slate tiles, which are available in many sizes and shapes, are wonderful for lining a shower stall or creating a tub surround. Some people choose to do the entire bathroom in stone, treating even the counters, walls, and floors with the rugged material. Limestone can

Opposite: HEAVY STONE WALLS PAINTED LINEN WHITE AND A LOW CEILING WITH EXPOSED BEAMS CREATE A COZY CAVELIKE FEELING IN THIS SMALL BEDROOM. TO INCREASE THE FEELING OF SPACE IN CLOSE QUARTERS, THE SAME OFF-WHITE COLOR IS USED FOR THE CURTAINS AND THE BEDSPREAD. Above: GLEAMING DARK BROWN MARBLE STREAKED WITH GRAY FITS PERFECTLY INTO THIS BATHROOM, WHERE THE FOCUS IS ON WORKS OF ART AND NOT ON THE CABINETS OR FIXTURES. HERE, THE DARK MARBLE DRAWS THE ATTENTION AWAY FROM ITSELF AND DIRECTS IT TOWARD THE OBJECTS IN THE ROOM.

be a beautiful choice, with its subtle blues and grays, but it is porous and therefore needs to be treated with a sealant before use.

Anything goes where color is concerned. Glossy black granite or cool white marble can be set off with minimalist chrome and glass fixtures and accessories for a sleek, sophisticated look. Warm taupe or beige travertine combines with shiny brass fixtures and dark wood cabinetry to lend an aura of traditional refinement to the bath. Marble and granite in rich reds and greens can heighten a mood of sensuousness and luxury. Even a rustic, old-world ambience can be created with these materials: choose slate or marble in earthy browns and beiges, or soft golden limestone with a weathered finish.

Above:. A RUGGED STONE WALL MAKES A DRAMATIC STATEMENT IN THIS ECLECTIC BEDROOM. NICHES HAVE BEEN CUT INTO THE WALL TO PROVIDE A PLACE FOR BOOKS, ELIMINATING THE NEED FOR A NIGHTSTAND. THE RICH DAMASK BED LINENS AND CURTAINS AND THE ORIENTAL RUG ADD A SENSE OF WARMTH AND LUXURY THAT COMPLEMENTS THE RUSTIC NATURE OF THE STONE AND STUCCO WALLS. **Opposite:** A CENTRAL LEADED-GLASS ROSE WINDOW SET INTO A GRAND ARCH CREATES A DRAMATIC FOCAL POINT FOR THIS BEDROOM. THE ARCH, FILLED WITH EXPOSED BRICK, HAS TWO MARBLE INSETS SYMMETRICALLY PLACED ON EITHER SIDE OF THE CIRCLE.

Opposite: This light, elegant bathroom has a full marble shower stall, marble wainscoting, and a marble floor. All the edges in the room, including the chair rail, have been ground to a rounded finish for both practical and aesthetic reasons. **Above:** Dark colors tend to shrink a room, but you can counteract this effect in different ways. In this bathroom, for example, the dark green marble walls and tub surround have a polished surface that is reflective even in low light situations. A tall mirror to one side of the tub reflects not just the available light but also the opposite side of the room, which makes the space appear larger.

Below: THIS TRAVERTINE TUB AREA LOOKS BEAUTIFUL BUT REQUIRES SPECIAL CARE. TRAVERTINE, A CHEMICAL LIMESTONE THAT RESEMBLES MARBLE WHEN POLISHED, COMES FROM THE EVAPORATION OF CALCIUM CARBONATE FROM FRESH OR SALT WATER. A GOOD HARD SCRUBBING CAN DESTROY THE SURFACE OF TRAVERTINE, WHICH SHOULD BE CLEANED WITH NOTHING STRONGER THAN A SPONGE AND WARM WATER.

Above: ONE WARM, NEUTRAL COLOR PREVAILS IN THIS REFINED MARBLE BATHROOM SET AMONG THE TREETOPS. THE MONOCHROMATIC COLOR SCHEME KEEPS THE FOCUS ON THE SPLENDID VIEWS AVAILABLE FROM THE WINDOWS AND THE DRAMATIC SKYLIGHT.

Above: SET INTO A MARBLE-CLAD CORNER, THIS CIRCULAR MOSAIC HOT TUB LOOKS WARM AND INVITING. A LACE-CURTAINED WINDOW WITH WOODEN TRIM, AN ANTIQUE WOODEN CHEST, AN OLD-FASHIONED MARBLE SCULPTURE, AND A LARGE FRAMED FLORAL TAPESTRY HELP TO GIVE THIS CONTEMPORARY SPACE A SENSE OF ANTIQUITY.

Opposite: ALTHOUGH THESE WALLS APPEAR TO BE MADE OF DRY, UNMORTARED STONES, THE MASONS CEMENTED THE STONES TOWARD THE BACK WHERE IT WOULDN'T SHOW. THIS ANCHORING KEEPS THE STONEWORK SAFE AND MAINTAINS THE ATTRACTIVE PATTERN OF HORIZONTAL LINES IN THIS LIGHT AND AIRY TUB ROOM. AN EXTERIOR STEPPED WALL CONTINUES THE PATTERN OUTDOORS WHILE BLENDING INTO THE LANDSCAPE. THE CONSISTENT USE OF STONE AND THE BROAD EXPANSE OF GLASS SEPARATING INDOORS FROM OUT MINIMIZE THE DISTINCTION BETWEEN THE TWO AREAS.

Right: POLISHED GRANITE IS AN EXCELLENT CHOICE FOR TUB SURROUNDS AND BATHROOM FLOORS BECAUSE ITS NONPOROUS SURFACE DOES NOT STAIN WHEN WET. IT IS PARTICULARLY SUITABLE FOR SEASIDE LOCATIONS, SUCH AS THIS BEAUTIFUL HOME, BECAUSE THE SALTY AIR CANNOT DAMAGE IT.

Below: THE PALE WOOD OF THE FORMAL VANITY WITH MOSAIC TILES BRINGS A FEELING OF LIGHTNESS TO THIS AIRY BATHROOM. A MOSAIC BORDER IN RICH, EARTHY COLORS ADDS WARMTH AND INTEREST TO THE ROOM, WHILE THE GLOSSY REFLECTIVE SURFACE OF THE TRAVERTINE COUNTERTOPS AND THE LARGE MIRRORS EMPHASIZE THE OPEN QUALITY OF THE SPACE.

Above: A MONOCHROMATIC SCHEME RUNS THE RISK OF SEEMING BLAND OR FLAT, BUT SUBTLE VARIATIONS IN HUE AND TEXTURE CAN MAKE A ONE-COLOR ROOM COME TO LIFE. IN THIS SPACIOUS BATH, SOFTLY PATTERNED MARBLE IN A RANGE OF TAUPES AND BEIGES ADDS DEPTH TO THE NEUTRAL PALETTE, WHILE PLUSH CARPETING, THICK TOWELS, AND A COMFORTABLE UPHOLSTERED CHAIR PROVIDE COMFORT AND WARMTH.

Opposite: THE CLEAN LINES AND STRONG EARTHY HUES OF MUSTARD, BRICK, AND BEIGE BALANCE THE VISUAL WEIGHT OF THE BROWN STONE TUB SURROUND, FLOOR, AND COUNTER. TEAL TOWELS ADD A SPLASH OF CONTRASTING COLOR, WHILE CHROME FIXTURES MAINTAIN THE BATHROOM'S SLEEK LINES. THE COUNTER SURFACE ADJACENT TO THE MIRROR IS THE PERFECT PLACE TO DISPLAY CONTEMPORARY CRAFTS LIKE THIS STRIKING VASE FILLED WITH FLOWERS.

DURABLE OUTDOOR DETAILS

For millennia, stone has been the material of choice for exquisite durable objects and architectural details inside and outside the home. Some early stone ornaments were made from *pietre dure*, hard semiprecious stones like agate, jasper, and lapis lazuli, cut with special gem-cutting tools. The Romans refined these ancient techniques, which experienced a second wave of popularity during the Renaissance. In the sixteenth century, Italian artists used *pietre dure* to create intricate mosaic panels for tabletops, cabinets, and other furnishings. The Florentines still make these pieces today.

Mantels, dresser tops, tables, lamp bases, and candlesticks made of marble are popular because they lend a touch of elegance to a room without requiring that the owner spend a fortune on the decor. Stone sculptures, urns, pedestals, fountains, birdbaths, and fossils can bring a sense of history to even the most modern room.

Outdoors, the creative use of stone can inject humor or mystery into a garden. With their cool, dark, damp interiors, stone grottoes recall the days of cave dwellers. Grottoes, however, often hold sophisticated surprises like mosaic floors, grotesque or humorous sculptures, a fountain or waterfall, and a place to sit and ponder the mysteries of life.

Whether formal or informal, stone patios carry the style of the house outdoors. Adorned with a jumble of flower-filled pots and comfortable chairs or benches, traditional flagstone or slate patios project warmth and cheerfulness. Colorful mosaics on a patio wall suit a Mediterranean-style villa, while a bold sculpture of either abstract or figurative design makes an effective ornament when set against the broad planes of a cubist house.

Stone can transform a common garden item into a substantial work of art. While a wooden arbor entwined

Opposite: WEATHERED STONE HAS BEEN USED HERE TO CREATE A POOL AND SURROUNDING PATIO WITH THE ELEGANCE AND TIMELESS QUALITY OF AN ANCIENT GREEK STRUCTURE. THE PALE STONE WALL OF THE POOL REFLECTS THE SUNLIGHT THAT COMES THROUGH THE WATER, CREATING A COOL, SPARKLING PLACE IDEAL FOR A MORNING SWIM BEFORE BREAKFAST. **Above:** MARBLE'S SOFTNESS ALLOWS IT TO BE CARVED IN GREAT DETAIL. THIS NATURALISTIC CARVING OF A FLOWERING STEM FROM THE TAJ MAHAL IN AGRA, INDIA, IS STARTLING IN ITS CLARITY AND REFINEMENT.

with vines blends into its surroundings, a granite arbor has a powerfully sculptural presence both in summer, when it might be covered with climbing roses or vines, and in winter, when it may be half buried in the snow.

Fountains made of stone can affect the garden's mood tremendously. Japanese-style gardens often include fountains made of uncut stone and bamboo, which appear to have come from nature rather than the hand of man, and have a strong, elemental presence. A traditional European garden, however, might have an ornate fountain carved with cherubs, dolphins, or young maidens bearing water pitchers. Modern designs include a glistening sheet of water sliding down a polished granite wall, and a contemporary construction using the force of water to turn stone spheres in a shallow stone basin.

By looking carefully at your rooms and gardens, you'll discover new uses for stone and marble around the house. Let these materials inspire you to create something distinctive and special. Whether you live in a castle or a cottage, stone and marble can transform your home in ways both subtle and dramatic.

Above: CARVED ACANTHUS LEAVES ENCIRCLE THE BASE OF THIS STONE BIRDBATH, SUPPORTED BY FOUR BRONZE TURTLES ON A CIRCULAR STONE PLATFORM. WHEN BUYING STONE GARDEN ORNAMENTS, IT'S IMPORTANT TO RESEARCH WHICH MATERIALS CAN SURVIVE THE CLIMATIC EXTREMES OF YOUR LOCATION. THE SAME MARBLE THAT LASTS FOR MILLENNIA IN SOUTHERN ITALY OR GREECE WOULD DISINTEGRATE IN THE SEVERE CLIMATE OF THE AMERICAN MIDWEST.

Above: THOUSANDS OF YEARS AGO, THESE MARINE CREATURES BECAME EMBEDDED IN ROCK. EVENTUALLY, THE ORGANIC MATERIAL WAS WORN AWAY, LEAVING A MOLD THAT GRADUALLY FILLED WITH LIMESTONE. THESE LIMESTONE CASTS HAVE ALL THE INTRICATE DETAILS OF THE ORIGINAL CREATURES, BUT THEY ARE SOLID STONE. FOSSILS SUCH AS THESE MAKE WONDERFUL DECORATIVE ACCENTS.

Opposite: A COARSE STONE WALL MAKES AN IMPOSING BACKDROP FOR THE SIMPLE BUT SOPHISTICATED FURNISHINGS ON THIS VERANDA. THE GREEN AND WHITE SOFA UPHOLSTERY LOOKS COOL IN CONTRAST WITH THE WARM STONE AND CLAY WALL, AND ITS PATTERNS OF CHECKS AND STRIPES BALANCE THE ORGANIC ELEMENTS INCLUDING THE WALL, THE WICKER FURNITURE, AND THE FLOWERS. **Above:** THIS IDYLLIC SCENE RELIES ON STONE FOR SUBSTANCE AND BEAUTY. THE COOL STONE PATIO, SET FOR AN ALFRESCO LUNCH, LOOKS PARTICU-LARLY INVITING UNDER THE SHADE OF THE GRAPE ARBOR. THE ROUGH EXTERIOR STONE WALL GIVES THE WHOLE SCENE A RUSTIC FEELING.

Left: STONE GIVES THIS TERRACE OVER THE SEA SUBSTANCE AND A SENSE OF PERMANENCE. ALTHOUGH THE SEATING IS LIGHTWEIGHT AND THE TABLETOP IS GLASS, THE MASSIVE BASE OF THE TABLE IS MADE OF CARVED STONE AND THE TERRACE FLOOR IS A PATCHWORK OF IRREGU-LARLY SHAPED PAVERS. IRREGULAR PAVERS ARE APPROPRIATE FOR AN IN-FORMAL LOOK, WHILE STRAIGHT-CUT STONES APPEAR MORE FORMAL.

Opposite: THE DESIGN OF THESE HANDSOME WALLS REFLECTS THE SHAPES AND COLORS IN THE SURROUNDING LANDSCAPE. VISIBLE IN THE DISTANCE IS A MESA, A FLAT-TOPPED ELEVATION, WHICH LOOKS LIKE IT WAS INTENDED TO BE AN INTEGRAL PART OF THIS SOUTHWESTERN LANDSCAPE.

Opposite: THIS LIMESTONE MERMAID SITS IN THE ALCOVE OF A WALL-LIKE HEDGE. STONE IS USED IN THIS GARDEN NOT ONLY FOR DECORATIVE REASONS BUT ALSO FOR PURPOSES OF LINE AND STRUCTURE. STONE STEPS DESCEND TO THE LOWER LEVEL OF THE GARDEN, AND ROUGH COBBLES SEPARATE THE PATH FROM THE PLANTING BED. **Above:** LAVISH VEGETATION SOFTENS THE HARD EDGES OF THE RUGGED STONE FACADE OF THIS HOUSE. LUSH PLANTS ALSO DIMINISH THE BRIGHTNESS OF THE WHITE STONE COPING AROUND THE POOL AND HELP TO BLEND IT INTO ITS SETTING. THE SELECTION OF COPING MATERIAL OFTEN DETERMINES HOW WELL A POOL ULTIMATELY FITS INTO ITS ENVIRONMENT.

Opposite: THE STONE HARDSCAPE AROUND THIS DECORATIVE POOL IS INTEGRATED INTO ITS SURROUNDINGS BY MEANS OF CAREFULLY SELECTED PLANT MATERIAL. PERENNIAL GRASSES AND FLOWERS NOT ONLY THRIVE IN THE WATER BUT ALSO GROW AROUND AND THROUGH THE STONE PAVING. BEHIND THE FORE-GROUND PERENNIALS IS A DENSE PLANTING OF SHRUBS AND TREES. A STONE FROG FOUNTAIN IS A WHIMSICAL ADDITION TO THE POOL. **Right:** GARDEN FURNITURE DOESN'T HAVE TO BE EXPENSIVE TO BE BOTH USEFUL AND ATTRACTIVE. IT CAN BE AS SIMPLE AS THIS TABLE, COMPOSED OF A SLATE SLAB RESTING ON LEGS MADE FROM LIMESTONE BLOCKS AND ARCHITECTURAL FRAGMENTS.

Above: STONE IS AN INDISPENSABLE ELEMENT OF A JAPANESE-STYLE GARDEN. HERE, A STONE LANTERN AND A FOUNTAIN CONSTRUCTED FROM A STONE BASIN WITH A BAMBOO SPOUT SIT AMONG NATURAL ROCKS HARMONIOUSLY ARRANGED ON A BED OF GRAVEL. LOW CONIFERS AND AZALEAS CONTRIBUTE TO THE PEACEFUL AND REFLECTIVE MOOD OF THE GARDEN. **Opposite:** THE MOSS THAT FILLS THE CREVICES BETWEEN THESE RECTANGULAR PAVERS EASES THE TRANSITION FROM THE SOLID FURNISHINGS TO THE LUXURIANT SHRUBS AND TREES BEYOND THE PATIO. IN THIS BUCOLIC SETTING, STONE IS THE UBIQUITOUS MATERIAL FOR CONSTRUCTION. THE WIDE CURVE OF THE STONE SETTEE ECHOES THE SHAPE OF THE STONE TABLE SET INTO THE PATIO. IRISES GROW IN THE SHALLOW STONE TROUGH ON THE TABLE.

Sources

**ARCHITECTS AND
INTERIOR DESIGNERS**

(pages 2, 30, 54 right)
Stone Wood
Sacramento, CA
(916) 454-1506

(page 17)
Henrietta Spencer-Churchill
Woodstock Designs
London, England
44 171-584 8576

(pages 25 right, 26, 28,
29)
Cathy MacFee
Lafayette, CA
(925) 254-2600

(pages 31, 32 left)
Kitchen Artworks
South San Francisco, CA
(650) 692-0843

(page 32 right)
Nancy Cooper
Santa Rosa, CA
(707) 542-7669

(page 35)
Kathleen & Doug Dale
Tahoe City, CA
(707) 583-0283

(page 36)
Diane Chapman
San Francisco, CA
(415) 346-2373

(pages 40, 42 right)
John Tobeler Design
San Francisco, CA
(415) 252-9400

(page 49)
Margaret Tiffin
London, England
44 171-584 8576

(page 50 left)
Werner Design Associates
Redwood City, CA
(650) 367-9033

(pages 50 right, 53)
Miller/Stein
Menlo Park, CA
(650) 328-1610

(page 54 left)
Acorn Kitchen and Bath
Oakland, CA
(510) 547-6581

(page 55)
Fu Tung Chang
Berkeley, CA
(510) 849-3272

(page 62)
Roger Harned
Bolinas, CA
(415) 868-1636

(page 67)
Jane Packer
London, England
44 171-486 5034

SUPPLIERS

Ann Sacks Tile & Stone
Portland, OR
(503) 281-7751
Website: www.annsacks.com

Country Floors
15 E. 16th Street
New York, NY 10003
(212) 627-8300

Sheldon Slate
Monson, ME
(207) 997-3615
Slate sinks, countertops,
vanities

Stone Forest
Department G
PO Box 2840
Sante Fe, NM 87504
(505) 986-8883
Hand-carved granite bird-
baths, basins, fountains,
lanterns, and spheres

Stone Legends
301 Pleasant Drive
Dallas, TX 75217
(214) 398-1199
Elegant cast stone products

Stone Magic
5400 Miller
Dallas, TX 75206
(214) 826-3606
Cast stone mantels, from classic to contemporary styles

PHOTOGRAPHY CREDITS
©**Antone Bootz:** pp. 6, 45

©**www.davidduncan-livingston.com:** pp. 2 (Designer: Stone Wood), 25 right, 26, 28, 29 (Designer: Cathy MacFee), 30 (Designer: Stone Wood), 31, 32 left (Designer: Kitchen Artworks), 32 right (Designer: Nancy Cooper), 35 (Designer: Kathleen & Doug Dale), 36 (Designer: Diane Chapman), 40, 42 right (Designer: John Tobeler Design), 50 left (Designer: Werner Design Associates), 50 right, 53 (Designer: Miller/Stein), 54 right (Designer: Stone Wood), 54 left (Designer: Acorn Kitchen and Bath), 55 (Designer: Fu Tung Chang), 62 (Designer: Roger Harned)

Esto Photographics:
©Peter Aaron: p. 16

©**Michael Garland:** p. 65 (Designer: Marylin Lightston)

©**Anne Gordon:** pp. 13, 19 right, 57

Franca Speranza: pp. 21, 52, 63; ©Nider: pp. 20, 48, 51; ©Yvan Travert: p. 8; ©Alain Weintraub: p. 34

©**Nancy Hill:** p. 41 (Sterling Design Associates)

Houses & Interiors:
©Roger Brooks: p. 24; ©Simon Butcher: pp. 37, 38; ©Steve Hawkins: p. 27; ©Sandra Ireland: p. 14 top; ©Chris Rose: pp. 12, 15; ©Verne: p. 25 left

Interior Archive: ©Fritz von der Schulenburg: pp. 9, 60 (Designer: Mimi O'Connell), 61 (Designer: Mimi O'Connell)

©**Tim Street-Porter:** pp. 10 (Designer: Tom Calloway), 22, 33 (Designer: Stefanos Polyzoidis), 56, 64, 66

Studio Giancarlo Gardin: pp. 44, 46, 47

Elizabeth Whiting & Associates: Tommy Candler: p. 11; Michael Dunn: p. 19 left; Andreas V. Einsiedel: pp. 17 (Designer: Henrietta Spencer-Churchill, Woodstock Designs), 49 (Designer: Margaret Tiffin); Tom Leighton: pp. 42 left, 59; Di Lewis: p. 67 (Designer/florist: Jane Packer); David Markson: pp. 14 bottom, 68; Dennis Stone: p. 39; Tim Street-Porter: pp. 23 (Designer: Annie Kelly), 69; Simon Upton: pp. 18, 43; Victor Watts: p. 58

INDEX